T0365821

THE NIGHT I TALKED WITH GOD

by Adrian Moran

Print information available on the last page.

Rev. date: 12/13/2018

To order additional copies of this book, contact:
Xlibris
1-888-795-4274
www.Xlibris.com
Orders@Xlibris.com

2

This book is dedicated to my children,

Tim, Lea, Nick, Briana, B.J. and Brandi.

One night while lying in my bed and

thinking of the day, I wondered why

I felt so bad when things don't go my way.

I thought about myself and why things are the way they are—I got up and out of bed and looked out at the stars.

"Hey God?" I said, and waited as my voice moved through the air. "I really need to talk with you, please let me know you're there."

Just then I saw a shooting star go flying

across the sky! I gasped and slowly

closed my eyes, I knew He was

close by!

"Oh, God," I said, "I just don't know why things don't go my way. I cannot understand so much of what I do and say."

"I get sad when I forget to be a friend,

or help my mom and dad. I'm so

ashamed and my heart breaks when I'm

told that I've been bad."

"You see, God, it is just so hard to
always do what's right. Even when
I try my best or give it all my might.
I think I'm doing something good and
end up doing something wrong."

"When I mess up, it's such a sight,

I feel I don't belong."

"Please take some time with me, dear

God, and come down from above,"

"Help me, Lord, to change my ways and

live my life with love."

"Thank you, God, for listening and giving me your time. I'm sorry for taking up so much, I bet no one's life is like mine."

"Good night," I said, "I love you."

Then I crawled back in my bed.

I closed my eyes and went right to sleep

when the pillow touched my head.

That night I had the greatest dream and saw Jesus by my bed, He came and sat right next to me and answered all I said.

He told me:

child, don't fret and worry about

everything you do, life is about learning

just how special I've made you.

Every person here on Earth chooses

their own trail, some will learn fast or

slow, but with God no one fails.

I am always here to help, if only you

will ask. I'll never give you too much

to do, just take it task by task.

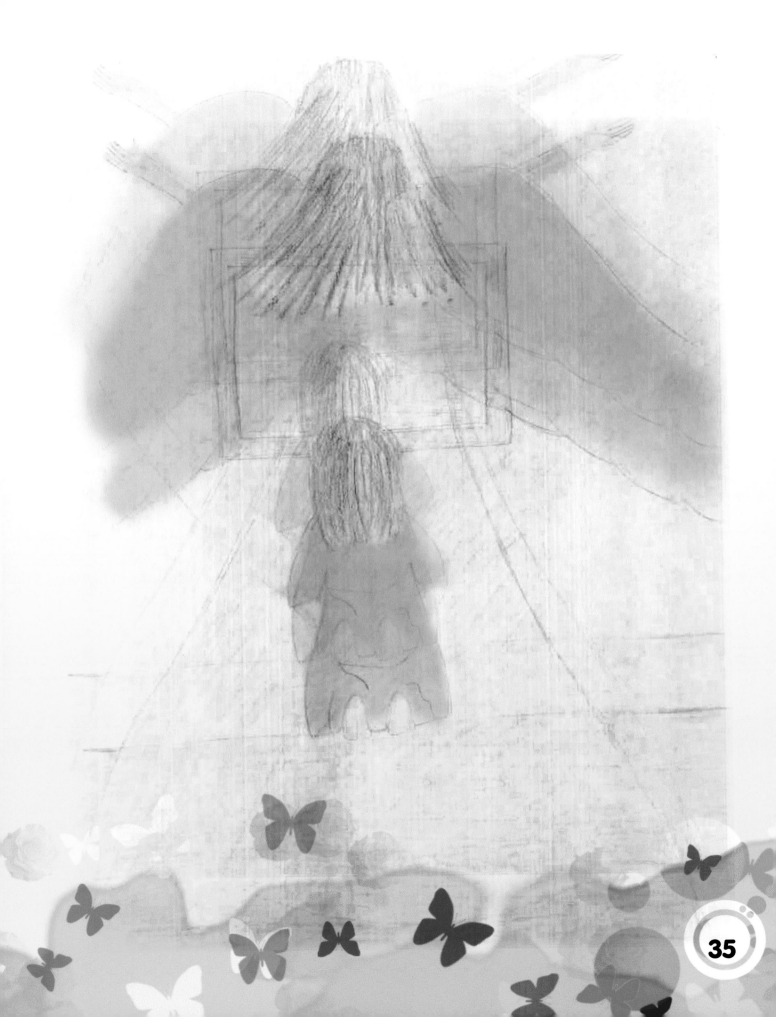

I love you so much I gave my life in payment for your sins. If you're sad or filled with doubt, open your heart and let me in.

I will show you the way and be your best friend in everything you do. I will be at your side from beginning to end because, child, I love you.

When I woke up and remembered the

dream, I was excited to start the day!

With God in my life and Jesus at my

Side, I will never lose my way!

The End.

Printed in the United States
By Bookmasters